Stress Lessening At Workplace

(Proven Strategies for Managing Stress in the Modern Office)

AVARY KINSMAN

Contents

Chapter One

Introduction: Understanding the Impact of Stress in the Workplace

Stress is a common problem that affects many people in the workplace. It can have a significant impact on an individual's physical and mental health, as well as their productivity and overall job performance. In this chapter, we will explore the causes and effects of stress in the workplace, and why it is important to take steps to manage and reduce it.

One of the main causes of stress in the workplace is a lack of control. People may feel that they have little control over their workload, deadlines, or the demands of their job. They may also feel that they have little control over the direction of their career or the company they work for. This lack of control can lead to feelings of powerlessness and frustration, which can contribute to stress.

Another major cause of stress in the workplace is a lack of support. People may feel that they do not have the support they need from their managers, colleagues, or family members. This can include a lack of feedback, recognition, or assistance with tasks. This lack of support can lead to feelings of isolation and insecurity, which can contribute to stress.

The effects of stress in the workplace can be significant. Stress can lead to physical symptoms such as headaches, fatigue, and muscle tension. It can also lead to mental health problems such as anxiety and depression. Stress can also lead to

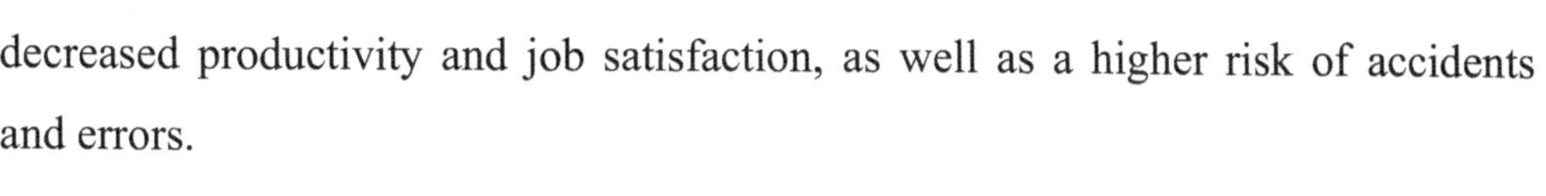
decreased productivity and job satisfaction, as well as a higher risk of accidents and errors.

It is important to take steps to manage and reduce stress in the workplace. By understanding the causes and effects of stress, and developing effective coping mechanisms, individuals can take control of their stress and improve their physical and mental health, as well as their productivity and overall job performance.

In conclusion, stress in the workplace is a common problem that can have a significant impact on an individual's physical and mental health, as well as their productivity and overall job performance. It's important to be aware of the causes and effects of stress and to take steps to manage and reduce it. This chapter sets the stage for the rest of the book and emphasizes the importance of stress management in the workplace.

Chapter Two

Identifying the Sources of Workplace Stress

In order to effectively manage and reduce stress in the workplace, it is important to first identify the sources of stress. These can vary from person to person, and may include a combination of internal and external factors. In this chapter, we will explore some common sources of stress in the workplace and how to identify them.

One common source of stress in the workplace is heavy workloads. This can include a large volume of work, tight deadlines, or a lack of resources to complete tasks. This can lead to feelings of pressure and overwhelm, which can contribute to stress.

Another common source of stress in the workplace is a lack of autonomy. People may feel that they have little control over their workload, deadlines, or the demands of their job. They may also feel that they have little control over the direction of their career or the company they work for. This lack of autonomy can lead to feelings of powerlessness and frustration, which can contribute to stress.

Conflict with colleagues or managers can also be a source of stress in the workplace. This can include disagreements over work assignments, communication breakdowns, or personality clashes. This can lead to feelings of tension and resentment, which can contribute to stress.

Work-life balance can also be a source of stress. People may feel that they have too much work and not enough time for personal or family commitments. This can lead to feelings of guilt and burnout, which can contribute to stress.

To identify the sources of stress in your workplace, it can be helpful to keep a stress diary. This is a journal where you record the events, situations, and feelings that are causing stress in your life. By keeping track of the situations that are causing stress, you can better understand the patterns and triggers of stress, and take steps to address them.

In conclusion, identifying the sources of stress in the workplace is an important step in managing and reducing stress. There are many potential sources of stress in the workplace, and it's essential to recognize them so that you can take steps to address them. By keeping a stress diary you can identify the patterns and triggers of stress. In the next chapter, we will explore some effective coping mechanisms to help you manage stress

Chapter Three

Developing Effective Coping Mechanisms

Once the sources of stress have been identified, the next step is to develop effective coping mechanisms to manage and reduce stress. Coping mechanisms are the strategies and techniques that individuals use to deal with the stressors in their lives. In this chapter, we will explore some effective coping mechanisms that can be used to manage stress in the workplace.

One effective coping mechanism is problem-solving. This involves identifying the problem, generating possible solutions, and implementing a plan of action. This can help individuals take control of the situation and feel more in control, which can reduce stress.

Another effective coping mechanism is time management and prioritization. This involves setting clear goals, breaking tasks down into smaller, manageable steps, and prioritizing the most important tasks. This can help individuals feel more organized and in control, which can reduce stress.

Mindfulness and relaxation techniques such as deep breathing, meditation, and yoga can be effective coping mechanisms for stress. These techniques can help individuals to focus on the present moment, and to let go of negative thoughts and feelings, which can reduce stress.

Exercise is also an effective coping mechanism for stress. Physical activity can help to release tension, improve mood, and boost self-esteem, which can reduce stress.

Effective communication is also a key coping mechanism for stress. By communicating effectively with managers and colleagues, individuals can address problems and conflicts, which can reduce stress.

In conclusion, developing effective coping mechanisms is an important step in managing and reducing stress in the workplace. There are a variety of effective coping mechanisms that can be used, such as problem-solving, time management, mindfulness and relaxation techniques, exercise, and effective communication. By utilizing these coping mechanisms, individuals can take control of the situation and feel more in control, which can reduce stress. In the next chapter, we will explore more specific techniques for building resilience and self-care to further combat stress

Chapter Four

Building Resilience: Mindfulness and Self-Care Techniques

In addition to developing effective coping mechanisms, building resilience and practicing self-care can also help individuals manage and reduce stress in the workplace. Resilience is the ability to bounce back from stress and adversity, and self-care is the practice of taking care of oneself physically, emotionally, and mentally. In this chapter, we will explore some specific techniques for building resilience and practicing self-care that can help individuals manage stress in the workplace.

One technique for building resilience is mindfulness. Mindfulness is the practice of being present in the moment and being aware of one's thoughts, feelings, and surroundings. It can help individuals to focus on the present moment and to let go of negative thoughts and feelings, which can reduce stress. Mindfulness can be practiced through different techniques such as meditation, deep breathing, or yoga.

Another technique for building resilience is positive self-talk. This involves replacing negative thoughts and beliefs with positive ones. This can help individuals to view stressors in a more positive light and to maintain a more optimistic outlook, which can reduce stress.

Self-care is another important technique for building resilience. This includes taking care of one's physical, emotional, and mental well-being. Some examples of self-care include: getting enough sleep, eating a healthy diet, taking regular breaks, practicing relaxation techniques, and engaging in hobbies and activities that bring joy.

It's also important to set boundaries and learn to say no to unnecessary tasks, meetings or request. This can help individuals to avoid becoming overwhelmed and to prioritize their time and energy on what's important.

In conclusion, building resilience and practicing self-care are essential for managing and reducing stress in the workplace. By practicing mindfulness and positive self-talk, and by engaging in self-care activities, individuals can improve their physical, emotional, and mental well-being, which can help them to better cope with stressors. By setting boundaries and learn to say no, individuals can avoid becoming overwhelmed and prioritize their time and energy on what's important.

In the next chapter, we will explore the importance of effective communication in managing stress in the workplace.

Chapter Five

Communicating Effectively with Managers and Colleagues

Effective communication is a key factor in managing stress in the workplace. By communicating effectively with managers and colleagues, individuals can address problems and conflicts, which can reduce stress. In this chapter, we will explore some strategies for effective communication in the workplace that can help individuals manage stress.

One strategy for effective communication is active listening. This involves paying attention to what others are saying, and responding in a way that shows understanding. By actively listening to others, individuals can build stronger relationships with their colleagues and managers, and can address problems and conflicts more effectively, which can reduce stress.

Another strategy for effective communication is assertiveness. This involves expressing one's own needs and wants in a clear and direct way, while still respecting the rights of others. By being assertive, individuals can communicate their concerns and needs effectively, which can reduce stress.

It's also important to communicate effectively with one's manager and team, this can be achieved by setting clear expectations, goals, and deadlines, and regularly checking in on progress. This can help to avoid confusion and misunderstandings, which can contribute to stress.

Effective communication also involves understanding and respecting different communication styles. This means being aware of and understanding the different ways that people communicate, and adapting one's own communication style to suit.

In conclusion, effective communication is a key factor in managing stress in the workplace. By communicating effectively with managers and colleagues, individuals can address problems and conflicts, and build stronger relationships, which can reduce stress. By actively listening, being assertive, setting clear expectations, understanding and respecting different communication styles, individuals can communicate their concerns and needs effectively, which can lead to better understanding and reduce stress. In the next chapter, we will explore the importance of time management and prioritization in managing stress in the workplace.

Chapter Six

Time Management and Prioritization

Effective time management and prioritization are essential for managing stress in the workplace. By setting clear goals, breaking tasks down into smaller, manageable steps, and prioritizing the most important tasks, individuals can feel more organized and in control, which can reduce stress. In this chapter, we will explore some strategies for effective time management and prioritization that can help individuals manage stress in the workplace.

One strategy for effective time management is setting clear goals. This involves identifying what needs to be done, and setting specific, measurable, and achievable goals for completing tasks. By setting clear goals, individuals can have a better understanding of what needs to be done, and can prioritize their time and energy on the most important tasks.

Another strategy for effective time management is breaking tasks down into smaller, manageable steps. This can help individuals to feel less overwhelmed by large and complex tasks, and to focus on one step at a time.

Prioritization is also an important strategy for effective time management. This involves identifying the most important tasks and focusing on them first. By prioritizing tasks, individuals can ensure that they are spending their time and energy on the things that are most important, which can reduce stress.

It's also important to understand the difference between urgent and important tasks, and to prioritize accordingly. Urgent tasks are those that require immediate attention and are usually time-sensitive, while important tasks are those that contribute to achieving long-term goals and objectives.

In conclusion, effective time management and prioritization are essential for managing stress in the workplace. By setting clear goals, breaking tasks down into smaller, manageable steps, and prioritizing the most important tasks, individuals can feel more organized and in control, which can reduce stress. By understanding the difference between urgent and important tasks, individuals can prioritize accordingly and ensure that they are spending their time and energy on the things that are most important, which can lead to better productivity and reduce stress. In the next chapter, we will explore the importance of creating a positive work environment in managing stress in the workplace.

Chapter Seven

Creating a Positive Work Environment

Creating a positive work environment can play a crucial role in managing stress in the workplace. A positive work environment can promote well-being, productivity and job satisfaction, which can help to reduce stress. In this chapter, we will explore some strategies for creating a positive work environment that can help individuals manage stress in the workplace.

One strategy for creating a positive work environment is fostering a culture of open communication. This means encouraging employees to share their ideas, concerns and feedback openly and freely. By fostering open communication, organizations can create a culture of trust and respect, which can promote well-being and reduce stress.

Another strategy for creating a positive work environment is promoting work-life balance. This means encouraging employees to take regular breaks, and to disconnect from work when they are off the clock. This can help to prevent burnout, and can promote well-being and reduce stress.

Promoting employee recognition and appreciation is also a key strategy for creating a positive work environment. This means recognizing and rewarding employees for their hard work and contributions. By promoting employee recognition and appreciation, organizations can create a culture of positivity and motivation, which can promote well-being and reduce stress.

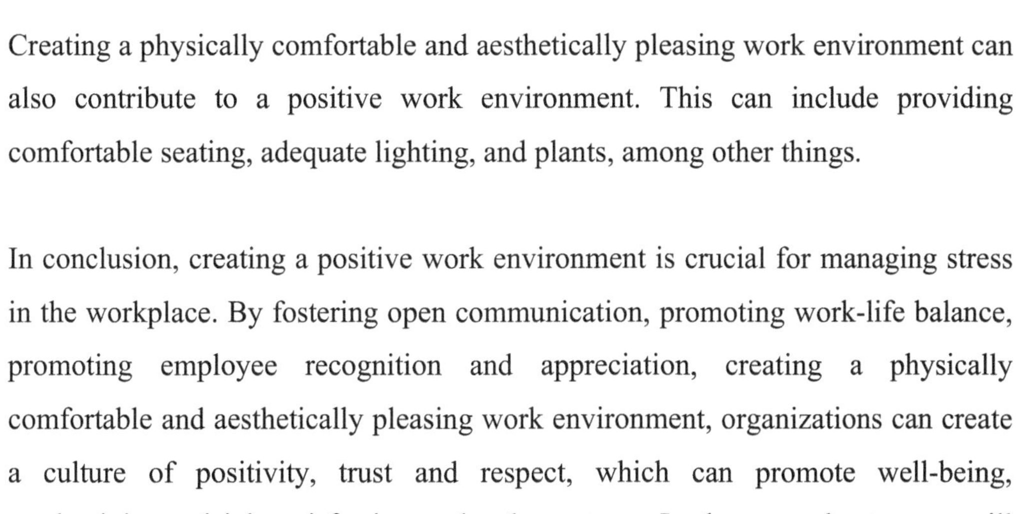

Creating a physically comfortable and aesthetically pleasing work environment can also contribute to a positive work environment. This can include providing comfortable seating, adequate lighting, and plants, among other things.

In conclusion, creating a positive work environment is crucial for managing stress in the workplace. By fostering open communication, promoting work-life balance, promoting employee recognition and appreciation, creating a physically comfortable and aesthetically pleasing work environment, organizations can create a culture of positivity, trust and respect, which can promote well-being, productivity and job satisfaction and reduce stress. In the next chapter, we will explore the unique challenges of managing stress in remote and virtual teams.

Chapter Eight

Managing Stress in Remote and Virtual Teams

In recent years, remote and virtual teams have become increasingly common in the workplace. While working remotely can have its advantages, it can also present unique challenges when it comes to managing stress. In this chapter, we will explore some strategies for managing stress in remote and virtual teams that can help individuals and organizations.

One strategy for managing stress in remote and virtual teams is to establish clear communication protocols and expectations. This means setting clear guidelines for communication, including how and when team members should communicate, and what types of communication are appropriate for different situations. By establishing clear communication protocols and expectations, team members can avoid confusion and misunderstandings, which can contribute to stress.

Another strategy for managing stress in remote and virtual teams is to foster a sense of community and connection among team members. This can be achieved through regular team meetings, virtual social events, and other activities that promote engagement and collaboration. By fostering a sense of community and connection, team members can feel less isolated and more supported, which can reduce stress.

It's also important to create a schedule and stick to it, this can include setting specific times for work, breaks, and leisure. This can help to maintain a sense of structure and routine, which can reduce stress.

Creating a comfortable and conducive work environment is also important for managing stress in remote and virtual teams. This can include ensuring that team members have access to the necessary tools and equipment, and that their home office is conducive to productivity and well-being.

In conclusion, managing stress in remote and virtual teams can present unique challenges, but by establishing clear communication protocols and expectations, fostering a sense of community and connection, creating a schedule, and creating a comfortable and conducive work environment, individuals and organizations can reduce stress and maintain productivity in remote and virtual teams. The next chapter will explore the stress that can come with change and transition in the workplace.

Chapter Nine

Navigating Change and Transition

Change and transition can be a major source of stress in the workplace. Whether it's a change in job responsibilities, a reorganization of the company, or a merger or acquisition, change and transition can bring uncertainty and instability, which can lead to stress. In this chapter, we will explore some strategies for navigating change and transition that can help individuals and organizations manage stress.

One strategy for navigating change and transition is to establish clear communication and transparency. This means keeping employees informed about the change or transition, and providing them with clear information about how it will affect them and their job responsibilities. By establishing clear communication and transparency, employees can feel more informed and in control, which can reduce stress.

Another strategy for navigating change and transition is to provide support and resources. This can include offering training and development opportunities, or providing access to counseling and employee assistance programs. By providing support and resources, employees can feel more supported and empowered to navigate the change or transition, which can reduce stress.

It's also important to acknowledge and validate employee's feelings, concerns and reactions to change and transition. This can help employees feel heard and understood, which can reduce stress.

Another strategy is to create a sense of continuity and consistency. This can include maintaining familiar routines, procedures, and processes as much as possible, which can help to reduce stress and uncertainty.

In conclusion, navigating change and transition can be a major source of stress in the workplace. By establishing clear communication and transparency, providing support and resources, acknowledging and validating employee's feelings, and creating a sense of continuity and consistency, individuals and organizations can better manage stress and support employees during change and transition. The next chapter will provide a conclusion on the topic and discuss the importance of sustaining a stress-free workplace culture.

Chapter Ten

Conclusion: Sustaining a Stress-Free Workplace Culture

Managing stress in the workplace is an ongoing process that requires ongoing effort and commitment. In this chapter, we will discuss the importance of sustaining a stress-free workplace culture, and provide some strategies for achieving this goal.

One key strategy for sustaining a stress-free workplace culture is to continue to identify and address the sources of stress. This means regularly assessing the work environment, and identifying and addressing any issues or concerns that may be contributing to stress. By continuing to identify and address sources of stress, organizations can stay ahead of potential problems and create a culture of proactive problem-solving.

Another strategy for sustaining a stress-free workplace culture is to continue to promote effective coping mechanisms and self-care practices. This can include providing regular training and development opportunities, and encouraging employees to take advantage of resources such as counseling and employee assistance programs. By continuing to promote effective coping mechanisms and self-care practices, organizations can help employees to manage stress and maintain their well-being.

It's also important to maintain open communication and transparency, and to involve employees in decision-making processes that may impact them. This can help employees to feel informed, included, and valued, which can reduce stress.

Another key strategy is to foster a culture of appreciation and recognition. This means recognizing and rewarding employees for their hard work and contributions, and creating a culture of positivity and motivation.

In conclusion, sustaining a stress-free workplace culture requires ongoing effort and commitment. By continuing to identify and address sources of stress, promoting effective coping mechanisms and self-care practices, maintaining open communication and transparency, involving employees in decision-making processes, and fostering a culture of appreciation and recognition, organizations can create a culture of well-being and productivity, which can help to reduce stress.

www.ingramcontent.com/pod-product-compliance
Lightning Source LLC
LaVergne TN
LVHW052115160826
845678LV00015B/3561

* 9 7 9 8 3 7 4 8 2 8 0 3 0 *